10

ARTWORKS
THAT CHANGED
THE WORLD

Written by Ben Hubbard

WAYLAND

www.waylandbooks.co.uk

First published in 2015 by Wayland
Copyright © Wayland, 2015

Editors: Julia Adams; Katie Woolley
Designer: Peter Clayman

Dewey number: 709-dc23
ISBN 978 0 7502 9136 1
Library eBook ISBN 978 0 7502 9137 8

Printed in China

10 9 8 7 6 5 4 3 2 1

Picture acknowledgements: Cover, p. 3 (4th from left), p. 23: © Neil Farrin/JAi/Corbis; p. 1, p. 25: © Ai Weiwei/Tate Photography; p. 2 (top), p. 3 (2nd from left), p. 17: © Succession Marcel Duchamp/ADAGP, Paris and DACS, London 2015; p. 2 (bottom, far left), p. 4 (top), p. 7: © Pierre Vauthey/Sygma/Corbis; p. 2 (bottom, 2nd from left), p. 9: © Leemage/Corbis; p. 2 (bottom, 3rd from left), p. 11: © Melvyn Longhurst/Corbis; p. 2 (bottom, 4th from left), p. 13 (main), back cover (top right): © Corbis; p.3 (far left), p. 4 (bottom), p. 14 (left-hand inset), p. 15, back cover (top left): © 91040/united archives/dpa/Corbis; p. 3 (3rd from left), p. 5, p. 21, p. 31: © 2015 The Andy Warhol Foundation for the Visual Arts, inc./Artists Rights Society (ARS), New York and DACS, London; p. 6: © Pierre Vauthey/Sygma/Corbis; p. 10: © Victor Fraile/Corbis; p. 12: © Atlantide Phototravel/Corbis; p. 13 (inset): © Stefano Bianchetti/Corbis; p. 14 (right-hand inset): © David Pollack/Corbis; p. 16: © Bettmann/Corbis; p. 18: © Underwood & Underwood/Corbis; p. 19, p. 30: © Succession Picasso/DACS, London 2015; p. 20: © Steve Schapiro/Corbis; p. 22: © Fred Prouser/Reuters/Corbis; p. 24: © Ai Weiwei/Tate Photography; p. 26 (top left): © Werner Forman/Werner Forman/Corbis; p. 26 (bottom right): © Universal History Archive/Getty images; p. 27 (top right and centre left): © The Gallery Collection/Corbis; p. 27 (centre right): © adoc-photos/Corbis; p. 28: © Stefano Bianchetti/Corbis; p. 29 (top right): © Corbis; p. 29 (centre right): © NASA/Roger Ressmeyer/Corbis; p. 29 (bottom left): © Sean Adair/Reuters/Corbis; p. 32: © Tom Grill/Corbis; all images used as graphic elements: Shutterstock.

Wayland, an imprint of Hachette Children's Group
Part of Hodder & Stoughton
Carmelite House
50 Victoria Embankment
London
EC4Y 0DZ

An Hachette UK Company
www.hachette.co.uk
www.hachettechildrens.co.uk

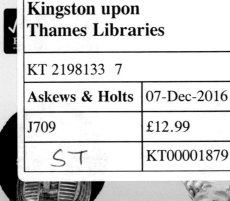

Contents

INTRODUCTION

The history of human beings can often be shown through the history of our art. Art, in turn, has also shaped our history. People have been creating artwork for tens of thousands of years. Our early ancestors illustrated the walls of their caves with the animals of the ancient world. Finding these paintings in modern times has altered our understanding of the past. As history wore on, the nature of our art changed. Art became less about depicting objects and more about making statements.

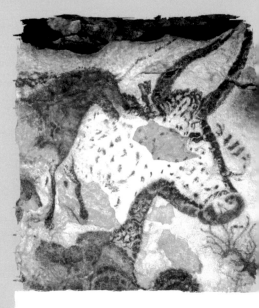

The Lascaux Cave Paintings (15,000 BCE) are among the world's oldest artworks.

Lord Kitchener Wants You (1914) urged men to join the army.

Beautiful artworks buried with mighty rulers showed off the wealth and power of ancient civilisations. Later, marble statues of biblical figures reminded people of the importance of religion in their society. This was art with a message, one that was designed to influence the way people thought. Before long, governments began using art as a political tool. Art as propaganda encouraged people to join in war efforts and urged young men to enlist in the army. Recruitment posters were responsible for vast numbers of men becoming soldiers during the First World War (1914–18). The destructive power of war was later depicted in the new art of the modern age.

Andy Warhol's *Campbell's Soup Cans* (1962) changed the way people saw art.

This new post-war art was abstract and surreal, and designed to change the world by changing people's feelings about it. It gave a voice to those who did not previously have one, and encouraged viewers to see things differently. Many modern artworks challenged people's thinking and created controversy. Soup cans, sunflower seeds and spray paint became the new art of the twentieth and twenty-first century. Often, this artwork made people ask, "What is art?". Answering this question is as difficult as choosing 10 pieces of art that changed the world. The list can only ever be based on one person's opinion. The 10 main artworks featured in this book are examples of how art has made us see, feel and think about things in certain ways. In doing so, art not only tells the story of human history – it helps create it.

THE LASCAUX CAVE PAINTINGS

In 1940, four teenage boys made an extraordinary discovery in Dordogne, France. By accident, they stumbled upon a hidden entrance to an ancient underground network of caves. Covering the cave walls were more than 2,000 paintings and engravings of animals, figures and symbols that had lain undisturbed for thousands of years. Archaeologists quickly closed off the site to investigate the artworks. Amazingly, they found that the images dated back to around 15,000 BCE, making them among the oldest known artworks in the world. People flocked to visit the art, which became known as the Lascaux Cave Paintings. But the breath from large numbers of visitors changed the climate in the caves and began to damage the artworks. Today, the paintings are closed off to the public once more.

PICASSO INSPIRED

Artist Pablo Picasso was so impressed by the Lascaux Cave Paintings that he remarked, "We have invented nothing", meaning modern art had not achieved anything new.

Today, only scientists preserving the paintings are allowed to enter the Lascaux Caves.

A section of the cave paintings, showing the now extinct aurochs bull.

Most of the Lascaux Cave Paintings show animals found in the local area, some of which are now extinct. Horses, deer, bulls, bison, birds, a bear and a rhinoceros were engraved, drawn and painted onto the walls. Some of the images are no bigger than a hand, others are taller than a man. A large painting of an aurochs bull is over five metres long. Using dyes found in local plants and pigments from the earth, many of the artworks have been painted in red, yellow, black, brown and violet. Instead of paintbrushes, these early artists used hair, pieces of moss and hollowed-out bones. Alongside the animals was one image of a human and some small, strange symbols.

15,000 BCE: EARLY PICTURES OF ANIMALS ARE PAINTED IN FRENCH CAVES ...

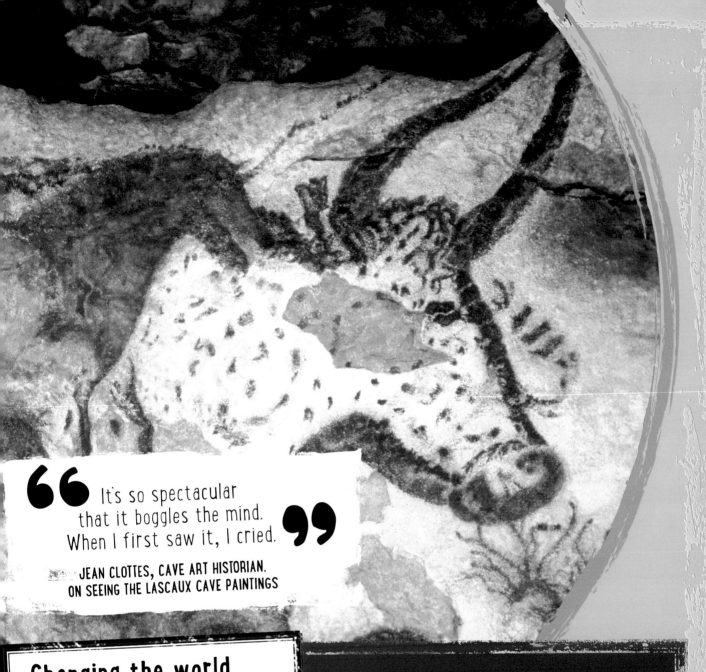

> **It's so spectacular that it boggles the mind. When I first saw it, I cried.**
>
> JEAN CLOTTES, CAVE ART HISTORIAN. ON SEEING THE LASCAUX CAVE PAINTINGS

Changing the world

Discovering the Lascaux Cave Paintings was a world-changing moment in our history and the history of art. In 15,000 BCE, early humans lived in caves, dressed in animal furs and hunted and gathered to survive. Nobody would have imagined that these early ancestors were also artists. However, these ancient people felt it was important to illustrate their world and the things within it. It was even more surprising that their artworks were far more than simple drawings of the things they saw. Their animals are shown jumping, running and twisting their necks. Each creature has been carefully watched and the movement of its body studied. It shows even the earliest people believed that creating art was an essential part of being human.

2014 CE: CAVE PAINTINGS OF ANIMALS FROM AROUND 37,000 BCE ARE FOUND IN INDONESIA

TUTANKHAMEN'S DEATH MASK

"As my eyes grew accustomed to the light, details of the room within emerged slowly from the mist, strange animals, statues, and gold – everywhere the glint of gold."

This is how archaeologist Howard Carter described finding the tomb of the ancient Egyptian pharaoh, Tutankhamen. Carter had been looking for the tomb for years without success and was about to give up the search. But then, in 1922, he found a flight of stairs which led to a tomb that had lain hidden for 3,000 years. The treasures inside included priceless jewellery, furniture, statues and clothes. However, the greatest prize of all lay within the coffin containing the pharaoh. Inside was the mummy of Tutankhamen, his face covered with a breathtaking solid-gold death mask.

A FLEETING PHARAOH

Over 150 gold amulets were found within the wrappings of Tutankhamen's mummy. Today, Tutankhamen is one of the most famous pharaohs in the world, even though he only ruled Egypt for around 10 years.

A masterpiece of Egyptian artwork, Tutankhamen's Death Mask was made from sheets of beaten gold, coloured glass and semi-precious stones. The mask was decorated with a striped headdress, black eye make-up and the ceremonial beard worn by both male and female pharaohs. The mask was stuck so fast to Tutankhamen's mummy, that Carter had to prise it off using a hammer and chisel. On the back, spells written in hieroglyphs asked the gods to safeguard the mask and its wearer. Tutankhamen's mummy was also buried with a gold vulture collar and amulets, designed to protect the pharaoh in the afterlife.

3100 BCE: ANCIENT EGYPTIANS BEGIN BURYING THEIR DEAD WITH ARTISTIC OBJECTS .

Tutankhamen died when he was about 18 years old, possibly from an infection caused by a broken leg.

Changing the world

Tutankhamen's Death Mask changed the world by giving modern people a haunting image of the pharaoh and his kingdom from beyond the grave. The mask was unlike any Egyptian artwork ever seen, before or after its discovery. The amazing craftsmanship of the mask and other burial items set the Western world alight with Egyptian fever in the 1920s. People were captivated by the wealth and power of an empire that could create such majestic treasures for a deceased pharaoh. From that point on, Tutankhamen's Death Mask came to represent the glory of ancient Egypt and our fascination with this extraordinary civilisation continues to the present day.

TERRACOTTA ARMY

One day in 1974, Chinese farmers digging a well struck a strange object buried in the soil. To their amazement, the farmers unearthed a life-sized terracotta statue of a soldier poised for battle. However, this statue was only the beginning of a world-changing discovery. Archaeologists called to the site soon uncovered 8,000 more soldiers in a series of large, underground pits. The soldiers were lined up according to rank and buried alongside hundreds of terracotta horses and more than 100 chariots. As the pits were excavated, it was found that the soldiers were part of a massive underground burial site. At the centre of the site was the tomb of Qin Shi Huang, an emperor from the third century BCE. It is thought that the Terracotta Army was stationed around the deceased emperor to protect him in the afterlife.

Although grey today, each soldier was originally painted to look as lifelike as possible.

> **66** I have a dream that one day science can develop so that we can tell what is here without disturbing the emperor, who has slept here for 2,000 years. **99**
>
> WU YONGQI, CURATOR OF THE TERRACOTTA ARMY MUSEUM

Archaeologists believe that the terracotta statues were produced along a type of assembly line, like modern cars today. However, once the bodies had been assembled, craftsmen went to work customising the statues. Individual moustaches, beards, hair, ears, noses and facial expressions made each statue unique. The soldiers were then painted in pink, red, brown, green, white and blue to make them look more lifelike. Buried for more than 2,000 years, this paint, along with the soldiers' wooden weapons, has long since been eaten away by the ravages of time.

246 BCE: WORK BEGINS ON EMPEROR QIN SHI HUANG'S TERRACOTTA ARMY...

It is thought around 700,000 labourers were used to construct the Emperor's tomb.

Changing the world

The Terracotta Army showed off the wealth and artistry of the Qin dynasty. It is the largest collection of pottery figures ever unearthed in China and one of the greatest archaeological discoveries worldwide. People were even more amazed to uncover that the Terracotta Army was only one part of an entire city of the dead that surrounds Qin Shi Huang's tomb.

The tomb itself is thought to be a life-sized model of the emperor's palace, containing terracotta figures of his government and courtiers. However, Qin's sealed tomb has been left undisturbed. The introduction of fresh air could destroy the paper, silk and paint painstakingly added to the figures in the creation of this extraordinary artistic masterpiece.

2012 CE: ARCHAEOLOGISTS DISCOVER THE EMPEROR'S TOMB IS INSIDE A WHOLE PALACE ...

MICHELANGELO'S
DAVID

In 1501, a little-known artist called Michelangelo began carving one of the most famous sculptures in human history. The result was *David* – a five-metre-high marble statue that is today considered one of the great masterpieces of Renaissance art. Yet it is only by luck that Michelangelo worked on the sculpture at all. Originally, the statue was one of several figures commissioned to sit on top of Florence Cathedral in Italy. After two artists dropped out of the job, the marble block for the statue lay untouched for 25 years. Luckily, 26-year-old Michelangelo was able to take over. Just over two years later, his statue was unveiled. However, it was too heavy for the cathedral roof and was instead installed outside the city's town hall, the Palazzo della Signoria. It took three whole days to transport the heavy statue half a mile from Michelangelo's workshop.

THE STATUE'S REPLICA

David was moved into the Gallery of the Academy of Florence in 1873 to protect it from the weather. A replica statue replaced the original outside the Palazzo della Signoria, later renamed the Palazzo Vecchio.

Once carved, David was too heavy for the Florence Cathedral roof.

Michelangelo's *David* was an instant hit among the people of Florence. The sculpture was unusual because it did not depict David standing over the defeated giant Goliath, which was common at the time. Instead, David is shown waiting for Goliath to appear. The statue looks thoughtful as he stands with his slingshot hanging over his shoulder, preparing himself for action. It is the way David stands, with his left leg bent and his torso slightly twisted, that many consider to be the genius of the artwork. Only a true master could portray the human body in such perfect detail.

The artist: Michelangelo di Lodovico Buonarroti Simoni.

Changing the world

Michelangelo was part of the Renaissance, or rebirth. This was a cultural movement that began in Florence, Italy. Renaissance artists took their inspiration from classical Greek and Roman sculpture and concentrated on creating realistic-looking people and creatures. To achieve this, artists such as Michelangelo studied and sketched bodies to recreate them accurately in their artworks. This enabled them to perfect small details that previous artists had struggled with. These details include the way people stand and move, and how their muscles look underneath their skin. This is why *David* amazed people when it was first unveiled and continues to do so today.

LORD KITCHENER WANTS YOU

Lord Kitchener Wants You is a First World War recruitment poster that encouraged British men to join the army. It was designed by graphic artist Alfred Leete, who never actually intended for the image to become a poster. Instead, he created the picture of Lord Kitchener, the British Secretary of State for War, for the cover of *London Opinion* magazine. However, when the government saw the cover it requested a recruitment poster be made from it. Recruitment posters urged young men to join the war by becoming soldiers. Over 10,000 copies of Leete's poster were plastered up around Britain in September 1914. This was also the month that the highest number of volunteers enlisted in the army.

Lord Kitchener Wants You inspired the later American *I Want You* war posters.

Leete's design was different from other war posters of the time, which usually only featured words. By using an image of Kitchener's pointing finger and staring eyes, Leete gave the poster a sense of drama. Kitchener appears to be staring straight out at the viewer and appealing to them directly. It was the simplicity of the words, combined with Kitchener's picture that made the poster such a powerful propaganda tool. Today, its groundbreaking graphic art still inspires modern designers.

> Posters appealing to recruits are to be seen on every hoarding, in most windows, in omnibuses, tramcars and commercial vans…Everywhere Lord Kitchener sternly points a monstrously big finger, exclaiming 'I Want You'.

THE TIMES NEWSPAPER, LONDON, 3 JANUARY, 1915

Changing the world

Lord Kitchener Wants You was one of many First World War propaganda posters that appealed to people to join the war effort. Other posters encouraged citizens to be thrifty, grow their own vegetables and not waste food. Recruitment posters urging men to enlist were used from the time of the Napoleonic wars, but *Lord Kitchener Wants You* set the benchmark for the modern age. It changed the world by showing governments could use the power of art to influence peoples actions. Art as a political tool was highly effective – many countries used a similar poster for their own army recruitment drives. The most famous example is the American *I Want You* posters, featuring Uncle Sam. Leetes poster has also inspired many humorous imitations that are used on t-shirts, cups, and even duvet covers that read 'Your Bed Needs You'. While Leete thought he was creating an eye-catching image for a magazine cover, he would never have believed his design would still be copied and celebrated more than 100 years later.

MARCEL DUCHAMP'S
FOUNTAIN

In 1917, Marcel Duchamp shocked and surprised the art world with something entirely different. His new piece was a white urinal, placed on its back, and signed 'R. Mutt'. Duchamp called the piece *Fountain* and submitted it to the Society of Independent Artists for an exhibition they were holding in New York, USA. According to the Society's own rules, any artist who paid a US$6 fee could have their artwork exhibited. The Society hoped that this would ensure new, interesting and daring art was given a chance to be shown to the public. But they drew the line at Duchamp's *Fountain*, because they did not consider art. *Fountain* was hidden from view at the exhibition and Duchamp resigned from the Society in protest.

GROUNDBREAKING ART

In 2004, Duchamp's *Fountain* was voted the most influential artwork of the twentieth century by 500 professionals from the British art world.

Duchamp was born in 1887 in Blainville, France, and became a US citizen in 1955.

Duchamp's *Fountain* was an everyday porcelain urinal made into an artwork simply by tipping it over and adding a false signature. It became one of Duchamp's 'ready-made' pieces, a term he coined for everyday objects used as art. His other ready-made artworks included the 1914 *Bottle Rack* and the 1913 *Bicycle Stool*, which consisted of a wheel mounted onto a stool. By selecting common objects as art, Duchamp wanted to challenge the idea of an artwork consisting of one unique piece. It worked. Although the original *Fountain* was lost, 17 replicas of the artwork exist in galleries around the world.

1917: DUCHAMP PAYS US$6 FOR HIS ARTWORK 'FOUNTAIN' TO BE EXHIBITED ....

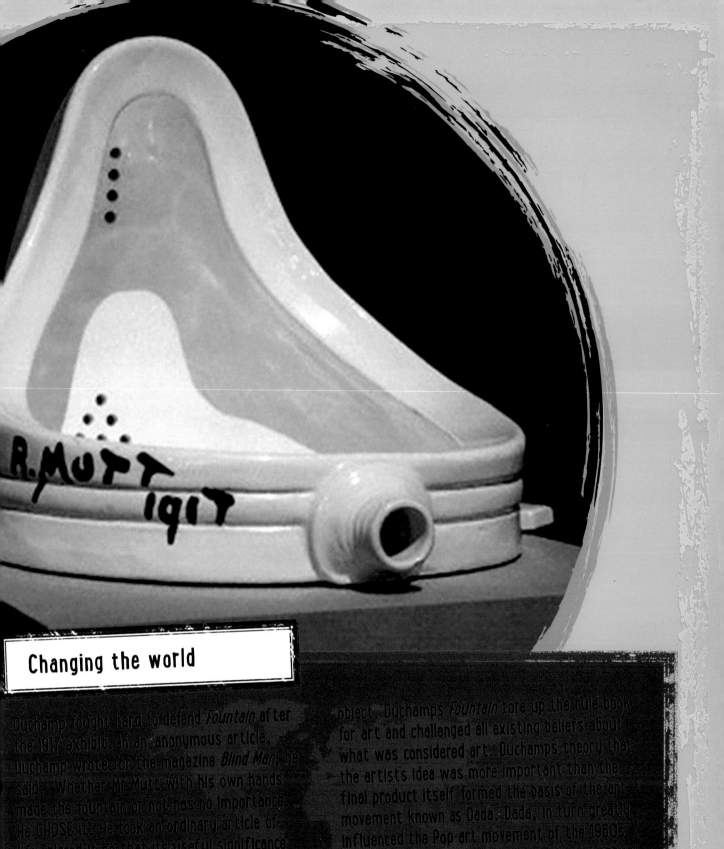

Changing the world

Duchamp fought hard to defend *Fountain* after the 1917 exhibit. In an anonymous article, Duchamp wrote for the magazine *Blind Man*, he said: 'Whether Mr. Mutt with his own hands made the fountain or not has no importance. He CHOSE it. He took an ordinary article of life, placed it so that its useful significance disappeared under the new title and point of view – and created a new thought for that object.' Duchamp's *Fountain* tore up the rule book for art and challenged all existing beliefs about what was considered art. Duchamp's theory that the artist's idea was more important than the final product itself formed the basis of the art movement known as Dada. Dada, in turn greatly influenced the Pop art movement of the 1960s and laid the foundation for all modern conceptual art that followed.

1999: A 1964 REPLICA OF 'FOUNTAIN' IS SOLD FOR US$1.7 MILLION .....

PICASSO'S *GUERNICA*

During the Spanish Civil War (1936–39), hundreds of citizens were killed during a Nazi bombing raid on the small town of Guernica in Spain. The 1937 bombing took place at the request of Spanish Nationalist Forces, who were fighting Republican soldiers in the area. A newspaper report of the bombing described the deaths of innocent men, women and children during the town's busy market day. After reading the report, Spanish artist Pablo Picasso picked up his paintbrush to bring the horrifying event to the attention of the world. He showed the resulting artwork, *Guernica*, at the 1937 Paris International Exhibition. The painting received little recognition until it toured across Europe and America in the years afterwards. There, it was met with great acclaim and brought the Spanish Civil War to the forefront of people's minds. However, Picasso would not allow the painting to be shown in Spain until democracy was restored to the country under a Republican government.

ARTWORK ARRIVES HOME

When *Guernica* arrived for the first time in Spain in 1981, the painting was visited by more than one million people. It was hung behind protective bullet-proof glass at the Casón del Buen Retiro in Madrid.

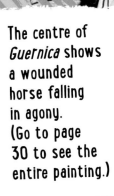

Picasso was born in Spain in 1881, but later lived in France.

Painted in shades of black, white and blue, *Guernica* appears like a giant black and white photo reporting the tragedy. The newspaper-type print running across the middle of the artwork adds to this reportage style. The painting shows death and destruction everywhere – a solider lies killed on the ground, a person is trapped by fire, and a mother cries over her dead baby. Standing at 3.5 metres high and nearly 8 metres wide, *Guernica* can be upsetting and it is a difficult painting to ignore.

The centre of *Guernica* shows a wounded horse falling in agony. (Go to page 30 to see the entire painting.)

1937: PICASSO'S 'GUERNICA' MAKES LITTLE IMPACT AT ITS UNVEILING ....

> **In the picture I am painting — which I shall call *Guernica* — I am expressing my horror of the military caste which is now plundering Spain into an ocean of misery and death.**
>
> PABLO PICASSO

Changing the world

Picasso painted *Guernica* to be seen by the thousands of people visiting the 1937 Paris International Exhibition. However, it was not in France but in England and America that the painting made people aware of the terrible events taking place during the Spanish Civil War. This created a large movement of people who were united in their condemnation of atrocities being committed by Spain's Nationalist army. Money made from exhibiting the painting was sent to help Spanish refugees, and the painting was finally gifted to the people of Spain in 1981. Today, it hangs in the Reina Sofía Museum in Madrid, and continues to be a symbol of the destructive power of war on the lives of innocent people. It also shows how art can create awareness of events and issues that are otherwise forgotten or ignored. This awareness is often the vital first step on the road to change.

WARHOL'S *CAMPBELL'S SOUP CANS*

When Andy Warhol created *Campbell's Soup Cans* in 1962, he was expecting controversy. But he could not have realised that the artwork would make him one of the most famous artists in the world. *Campbell's Soup Cans* is an artwork made up of 32 individual paintings that show the different flavours of Campbell's soup. When the artwork was first shown in California, USA, it caused a great stir in the art world. Many people simply hated it. Some criticised Warhol for depicting a product found in supermarkets as art. Others defended Campbell's artwork as legitimate art. The debate over this new art form, called Pop art, created great publicity for Warhol. He soon became America's best-loved Pop artist and could command more money for his works than any other living artist from the USA.

Andy Warhol directs a movie in his studio, The Factory.

Warhol created *Campbell's Soup Cans* by using silk-screening, a printmaking method often used in commercial art. Using stencils, Warhol repeated the same basic soup can image on each of the 32 canvases. He then hand-painted the different flavours of soup on to the can labels. When the cans were first exhibited together, they were placed on shelves. This gave the 2.5-metre high and 4-metre wide artwork the effect of being in a giant supermarket. As Warhol left no instructions about how his cans should be installed, they were displayed according to the year each soup was introduced to the market. The first flavour introduced by Campbell's was tomato, in 1897.

1962: ANDY WARHOL'S 'CAMPBELL'S SOUP CANS' ARE CRITICISED FOR NOT BEING AR

GREEN PEA SOUP

SCOTCH BROTH (A HEARTY SOUP) SOUP

VEGETABLE SOUP

CREAM OF ASPARAGUS SOUP

Old-fashioned TOMATO RICE SOUP

CREAM OF CELERY SOUP

CHILI BEEF SOUP

VEGETABLE BEAN SOUP

CREAM OF CHICKEN SOUP

> 66 I used to drink it. I used to have the same lunch every day, for twenty years, I guess, the same thing over and over again. Someone said my life has dominated me; I liked that idea. 99
>
> ANDY WARHOL, SPEAKING ABOUT CAMPBELL'S SOUP

Changing the world

Andy Warhol was at the forefront of the changing art world of the 1960s. His Pop art used everyday objects and subjects from popular culture and presented them to the world as art. Often, each artwork contained large, multiple copies of one thing, such as soup cans or coca cola bottles. His idea was to draw attention to objects from the commercial world that people often took for granted. He did the same for famous people, including film star Marilyn Monroe. Fascinated with celebrities, Warhol once said that everybody has 15 minutes of fame. *Campbell's Soup Cans* changed art, it changed the way people think about art, and today it is considered one of the greatest pieces of art of the twentieth century. Its legacy has ensured that Warhol's own fame has lasted far beyond the artist's death in 1987.

996: THE 32 PAINTINGS ARE SOLD TO MUSEUM IN NEW YORK FOR US$15 MILLION

BANKSY'S *SWEEPING IT UNDER THE CARPET*

Under the cover of darkness one night in 2006, graffiti artist Banksy got to work on a wall along a street in north London. By morning, passers-by could see his new mural *Sweeping it Under the Carpet*. The mural, which showed a maid lifting the wall to sweep underneath it, was painted over completely by 2008. Having his artwork painted over, destroyed, or stolen is a common occurrence for the anonymous artist known as Banksy. Graffiti is a type of art that paints words and pictures in public places. It is illegal, so is often washed away or concealed with white paint. But Banksy's famous murals are also often carefully removed from walls and sold for high prices. *Sweeping it Under the Carpet* was estimated to be worth around £200,000 before it was painted over.

ARTWORK STATS

Created: 2006

Location: On a wall along a street, Chalk Farm, London

In 2007, *Sweeping it Under the Carpet* reappeared, this time on a wall of the London art gallery The White Cube. It was painted over within one month.

The live, painted elephant at Banksy's *Barely Legal* exhibition.

Using stencils and spray paint, Banksy usually works in the dead of night and targets walls and buildings in high profile areas. His artworks combine humour with social messages, which are often highly critical of governments, groups and individuals in the seats of power in modern society. They also poke fun at ordinary people who seem unwilling to create change. *Sweeping it Under the Carpet* was thought to be about the reluctance of Western governments to tackle important issues in poor countries, such as the AIDS epidemic in Africa.

Changing the world

Sweeping it Under the Carpet made people ask an age-old question, 'Is graffiti art?'. Graffiti is thousands of years old and divides popular opinion. Two thousand years ago, the ancient Romans painted graffiti of their emperors and gladiators. Today, tag lettering is sprayed everywhere on our modern city walls and is often removed. However, unlike other common forms of graffiti, there is usually outrage when Banksys murals are washed away or painted over. For many, Banksys graffiti is important, attractive and thought-provoking art. His work also fetches high prices and is exhibited in galleries across the globe. In this way, Banksys murals have changed the world – they have helped to make graffiti an accepted art form. Banksy himself has suggested his work is like a record of our time, similar to the Lascaux Cave Paintings painted in 15,000 bce. Maybe Banksys work will show future generations how the people of today felt about the modern world.

AI WEIWEI'S *SUNFLOWER*

Sunflower Seeds was an artwork by Ai Weiwei, who was imprisoned in a Chinese jail while it was being exhibited in 2011. The artwork united people around the world in their call for the artist's release. Ai Weiwei and his team created the installation artwork of 100 million porcelain sunflower seeds for an exhibition at London's Tate Modern. The seeds were spread across the gallery's Turbine Hall and visitors were invited to walk over them. In China, sunflower seeds are a common street snack that Ai Weiwei often ate during his childhood. At that time, millions suffered hunger and hardship during the country's Cultural Revolution. Sharing sunflower seeds became a welcome break from the poverty and uncertainty that surrounded people's everyday lives.

Ai Weiwei was born in 1957 in Beijing, China.

Ai Weiwei's *Sunflower Seeds* was deliberately created to trick the eye. From a distance, the artwork looked like a pile of identical seeds. But up close, the viewer could see that each seed was different – in fact, each one had been individually crafted. The seeds were made in Jingdezhen, the city where China's best porcelain was made for over 1,000 years. Here, it took 1,600 artisans over two years to create the porcelain seeds. During the 30-step process, each seed had to be fired in a 1,300-degree kiln and then hand painted. The result was 100 million unique seeds that all looked the same when put together in a pile.

2008: AI WEIWEI HELPS DESIGN CHINA'S OLYMPIC BIRD'S NEST STADIUM ...

> 66 From a very young age I started to sense that an individual has to set an example in society. Your own acts and behaviour tell the world who you are and at the same time what kind of society you think it should be. 99
>
> **AI WEIWEI**

Changing the world

When the Tate Modern commissioned *Sunflower Seeds*, Ai Weiwei was a popular artist who had been an artistic consultant on China's Olympic Bird's Nest stadium. But in 2011, he was imprisoned for criticising the Chinese government's human rights policies. The Tate Modern, which was showing *Sunflower Seeds* at the time, was one of thousands of organisations and individuals worldwide that called for Ai Weiwei to be freed. As well as articles, petitions and protests, huge donations were made to pay for his legal fees. In this way, *Sunflower Seeds*, an artwork about the importance of the individual within a crowd, also showed how a crowd can work together to help an individual. It once again proved the power of art in uniting people and bringing about change. Ai Weiwei once compared his *Sunflower Seeds* to the strength of the Chinese people by saying, "Seeds grow the crowd will have its way, eventually." He was freed from jail after almost three months.

2011: AI WEIWEI IS IMPRISONED AFTER CRITICISING THE CHINESE GOVERNMENT...

10 OTHER ARTWORKS THAT CHANGED THE WORLD

1. *Standard of Ur*

In about 2,600 BCE, a decorated wooden box was made in the Sumerian city of Ur, one of the first cities in the world. The box is covered with shells, lapis lazuli and marble only made in countries hundreds of miles away. It shows the wealth, trading ability and power of one of the first known kings. The king is shown on the box ruling over his subjects and conquered enemies.

2. *Assyrian Bas Relief*

The Assyrian Bas Relief is a wall relief showing the Assyrian army's massacre of the people of Lachish in around 650 BCE, It decorated the outside of the palace of Assyria's King Sennacherib. The relief is one of the first known propaganda artworks, serving as a warning to any visitors who might oppose the Assyrians.

3. Exekias' *Vatican amphora*

In about 540 BCE, the potter Exekias created a vase showing the famous black-figure decoration of ancient Greek pots and vases. Greek vases such as this one gave modern historians much information about the great Greek civilisation and their beliefs. The *Vatican amphora* depicts Achilles and Ajax, the heroes of the Trojan War, playing a board game.

4. *Portrait of the Baker, Terentius Neo and his wife*

A fresco discovered in the ancient Roman city of Pompeii, Italy, which lay covered in a thick layer of volcanic ash for nearly 1,700 years, gave an insight into everyday Roman life in the first century CE.

5. The *Bayeux Tapestry*

Thought to be the last surviving example of medieval embroidery, this tapestry is one of the only surviving pictorial records of the 1066 Battle of Hastings. Hastings was a landmark battle in the history of Britain and started the invasion of the country by the Normans.

6. The *Mona Lisa*

One of the most famous artworks of all time, the *Mona Lisa* was painted by Leonardo da Vinci in the early sixteenth century. It is considered the greatest painting of the Renaissance and set a benchmark for all fine art that followed. The *Mona Lisa* continues to be one of the most visited artworks in the world at its home in the Louvre museum in Paris, France.

7. *The Card Players* (1890s)

The Card Players are a series of five paintings made by French painter Paul Cezanne during the 1890s. They rocked the world by becoming some of the most valuable paintings in history. One version of *The Card Players* became the most expensive artwork ever in 2011 when it was sold for nearly US$300 million.

8. Dürer's *Rhinoceros*

Dürer based his 1515 *Rhinoceros* woodcut on eyewitness reports of a rhinoceros. As no rhinoceros had been seen in Europe for over 1,000 years, Dürer's portrait was completely inaccurate. However, it was often used as a true representation of a rhinoceros up until the eighteenth century. It is said that "probably no animal picture has exerted such a profound influence on the arts".

9. Jackson Pollock's *No.5*

This artwork is one of Pollock's best known examples of his 'paint drip' style, which included dribbling, dripping and splattering paint across a canvas. The style revolutionised the world of art, and forever changed how people defined it.

10. Tracey Emin's *My Bed*

My Bed is a Tracey Emin installation artwork which shows her bed and her bedroom objects around it. Condemned by critics in 1998 for not being art, the controversial piece was first shown at London's Tate Modern, and was sold in 2014 for £2.2 million.

TIMELINE

40,000 BCE
Early humans begin creating the first known artworks during the last ice age of the world.

15,000 BCE
The ancient dwellers of Lascaux in Dordogne, France adorn their caves with over 2,000 paintings of people and animals, giving an artistic interpretation of their stone-age world.

9000 BCE
An artwork of two figures is carved from pebbles near Bethlehem in the Middle East.

1323 BCE
The body of Tutankhamen, the boy king of Egypt, is laid to rest in an underground burial complex full of treasures, including his gold death mask.

1914
Start of the First World War.

1914
A poster of British Secretary of State Lord Kitchener saying "I want you" becomes a powerful First World War recruitment and propaganda tool.

1789
An angry mob storm the Bastille fortress and prison in Paris, which starts the French Revolution.

1917
Duchamp's *Fountain* is submitted for an exhibition in New York, USA. It is rejected by the exhibitors, is submitted for an exhibition in New York, USA. It is rejected by the exhibitors.

1937
Picasso unveils *Guernica*, a surrealist painting that acts as a statement about the Spanish Civil War bombing of the village that bears its name.

2010
Chinese artist Ai Weiwei's *Sunflower Seeds*, made from 100 million individually crafted porcelain pieces, is created for the Tate Modern in London.

2007
Painted on the outside wall of London's White Cube gallery, graffiti artist Banksy's *Sweeping it Under the Carpet* mural is painted over a few weeks later.

2007
Hirst's *For the Love of God* is given a £50 million price tag, making it the most expensive artwork by a living artist.

209 BCE
A terracotta army of more than 8,000 soldiers, 130 chariots and 520 horses are buried with Chinese emperor Qin Shi Huang.

476 CE
Roman Emperor Romulus Augustus is deposed by Germanic chieftain Odoacer, marking the beginning of the decline of the Roman Empire.

1215
The feudal barons of England sign the Magna Carta with King John, limiting his powers and setting out a new law of the land.

1766
Thirteen American colonies sign the Declaration of Independence which proclaims they are no longer part of the British Empire but instead a new 'United States of America'.

1504
A masterpiece of Renaissance sculpture, Michelangelo's statue of the biblical figure David is unveiled in Florence, Italy.

1492
Christopher Columbus lands in the Bahamas and begins his discovery of the Americas for Europe.

1939
Start of the Second World War.

1962
Andy Warhol's first solo exhibition in Los Angeles opens with his *Campbell's Soup Cans*, 32 printed screens. which dress up advertising as a form of art.

1969
Neil Armstrong becomes the first human to set foot on the Moon.

2001
Islamic terrorist group Al-Qaeda hijack four places in an attack on the Unites States that includes the destruction of the World Trade Center skyscrapers in New York.

GLOSSARY

abstract A type of art that does not show reality.

AIDS A disease affecting the immune system that is caused by a virus.

amulet A piece of jewellery thought to protect against disease, evil or danger.

ancestor A person from whom someone is descended.

archaeologist Someone who studies history by examining the objects and buildings left behind.

assembly line A manufacturing process whereby a product is pieced together gradually by different workers and machines as it passes along a production line.

atrocity A cruel and horrifying act that often causes injury or death.

canvas The cloth stretched over a frame to be painted onto.

climate Weather conditions in an area.

commission An order for a work of art to be specially made.

condemnation To disapprove of something.

controversy An argument between many people who disagree about something.

courtier A companion to a king or queen.

Cultural Revolution A period of political upheaval in China between 1966 and 1976, led by communist leader Mao Zedong.

dynasty A line of rulers who inherit the throne.

engraving A piece of art carved on to a hard surface.

enlist To enroll in the armed forces.

epidemic The spread of an infectious disease.

excavate To dig up something from the earth.

extinct To no longer be in existence.

fresco A type of painting done on a wall or ceiling.

graffiti Words or drawings painted on a public wall or building.

hieroglyph A picture that represents a word.

lapis lazuli A bright, blue rock used in jewellery.

mural A large artwork painted directly on to a wall.

Nationalist A supporter of political independence for their country.

pharaoh A ruler of ancient Egypt.

pigment A substance that colours something. For example, paints are made up of pigments.

Pop art An art movement that uses images from comic books, advertising, consumer products and television as art.

porcelain A white ceramic commonly used in bowls and cups.

printmaking Making multiple pictures or designs by printing from specially prepared plates or blocks.

propaganda The organised spread of certain ideas even if they are untrue, often during times of war.

recruitment The act of enlisting people into the armed forces.

refugee A person who has been forced to leave their country, often as a result of war.

relief A method of moulding or carving in which the design stands out from the surface.

Renaissance The revival of classic art and literature in the fourteenth to sixteenth centuries.

Republican A supporter of a republican government, who believes power should be held by the people and their elected representatives.

Spanish Civil War A conflict that began in 1936 between Nationalist forces and Republican forces and ended in the Nationalist government of General Franco, which stayed in power until 1975.

surreal A type of art that seeks to portray images from the unconscious mind.

terracotta A type of fired clay used to make statues and pottery.

thrifty To not be wasteful.

torso The trunk of a human body.

Uncle Sam A character that stands for the American government.

FURTHER INFORMATION

Books

In the Picture with... [series], by various authors, Wayland (2014)

The World in Infographics: Art and Entertainment, by Jon Richards and Ed Simkins, Wayland (2013)

Websites

The Tate Modern: http://kids.tate.org.uk

The National Gallery of Art: www.nga.gov/content/ngaweb/education/kids.html

Museum of Modern Art: www.moma.org/learn/kids_families/index

Places to Visit

Tate Modern: Bankside, SE1 9TG, London

Scottish National Gallery of Modern Art: 75/73 Belford Road, EH4 3DR, Edinburgh

Museum of Modern Art :The Tabernacle, Heol Penrallt, Machynlleth, SY20 8AJ, Powys

Apps

Museum of Modern Art Lab: https://itunes.apple.com/us/app/moma-art-lab/id529886963?mt=8

Louvre Museum Official App: http://appcrawlr.com/ios/musee-du-louvre

INDEX

DISCOVER MORE ABOUT WHO AND WHAT HAS CHANGED THE COURSE OF HUMAN HISTORY!

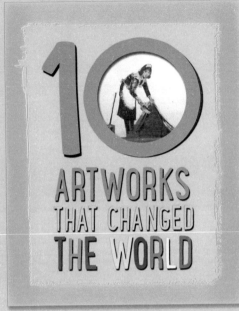

9780750291361

9780750291279

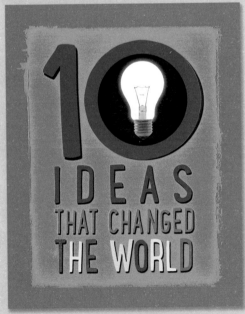

9780750291392

9780750291293

WAYLAND
www.waylandbooks.co.uk